قاعدة في الصبر

THE PRINCIPLE OF PATIENCE

IBN TAYMIYYAH

Qadeem Press

Qadeem Press

Qadeem Press Edition
Breathing Life into Forgotten Pages
www.qadeempress.com

Reprinted by Qadeem Press in 2026

Find our titles on your favourite online bookstore using the keyword 'Qadeem Press'

If you have questions regarding this edition, its source, or its publication status, please contact us @ ***info@qadeempress.com*** *or via our twitter handle* ***x.com/qadeempress.***

Translator's Preface

All praise is due to Allah, and may His peace and blessings be upon Muhammad, his believing household, and Companions. As for what follows:

Abū al-ʿAbbās Taqī al-Dīn Aḥmad ibn ʿAbd al-Ḥalīm ibn ʿAbd al-Salām al-Ḥarrānī, better known to the world as Shaykh al-Islām Ibn Taymiyyah, died at the age of 67, having spent his entire life serving Islam and its sciences.

He spoke the truth as he saw it, after careful investigation of the Qurʾān, Sunnah, and statements of the Imams of the Salaf, and he would issue fatwas and author books based on them. His enemies and enviers did their utmost best to vilify him before the leaders of the time and accuse him of various blasphemies and transgressions in the religion. As a result of their schemes, Ibn Taymiyyah was imprisoned on seven occasions and served sentences which totalled approximately five years and some days across the last 35 years of his life (693-728 A.H.). It was also in prison, that his soul was returned to its Maker. His student, Ibn ʿAbd al-Hādī, states:

> The period of his (final) sickness was 10 or so days and most people were unaware of it and so they were not taken by surprise except on hearing his obituary, after which there was severe sorrow and

abundant crying and sadness; his close relatives and companions entered his (cell) and the people crowded the gate of the fortress (where he was imprisoned) and its pathways, the Central Masjid of Damascus was full and they prayed over him and carried him (to his grave) over their heads. May Allah have mercy on him and be pleased with him.

Ibn Taymiyyah's funeral was attended by some 10,000 or so people a sign and attestation to his greatness and his acceptance among the people of knowledge and the people in general. And in this respect, Imam Ahmad reportedly said:

> Say to the people of innovation: between us, and you is the day of funerals!

Although Ibn Taymiyyah was imprisoned so many times, he was never dismayed and continued to call to the truth even if it was at the expense of the people's pleasure, He was a prisoner content with his Lord's decree, patient with what befell him, and cognisant of the hidden blessings of being imprisoned for nothing but a true and righteous cause.

During the year 709 A.H., Ibn Taymiyyah was released from the prison in Egypt and honoured by Sultan Nāşir, who had been absent from Egypt and was unaware of what had transpired regarding his imprisonments. The

Sultan sat with Ibn Taymiyyah in private and showed him some fatwas written by his enemies stating that he should be executed. The Sultan offered to execute some of Ibn Taymiyyah's enemies as a punishment for their transgression against him, but instead of taking revenge, Shaykh al-Islām praised them and said:

> If they are gone, you will never find in your land those who are similar to them. As for me, then they are acquitted with respect to my right and my own self.

This indicates Ibn Taymiyyah's tremendous tolerance over his enemies and his mercy for them. By pardoning them, he managed to save their lives. When this news reached Qādī Ibn Makhlūf al-Maliki, Shaykh al-Islam's nemesis, he said:

> We have not seen anyone more forgiving than Ibn Taymiyyah (from the people). It was not possible for us to carry out our efforts regarding him, but when he was able over us, he pardoned us.

Ibn Taymiyyah's most illustrious student Ibn Qayyim, who was jailed alongside his teacher during his final imprisonment, stated:

> And Allah knows that I did not see anyone live a purer life than him ever... despite what he suffered

from imprisonment, restraint and exhaustion, he was from the purest of people in living and most open-hearted, strong-hearted and most self-contented; the brightness of delight showed on his face.

Ibn Qayyim also relates the following famous words uttered by Shaykh-ul-Islam during his imprisonment:

> What can my enemies do to me? My Paradise and Garden are in my heart, wherever I go they are with me, they never separate from me. My imprisonment is a spiritual retreat. Killing me will be. martyrdom and removing me from my land is tourism.

Such was his contentment with his Lord's decree that he viewed imprisonment, rather all trials, as a blessing. He said:

> Allah has opened to me in this fortress during this time (deeper) meanings from the Qurʾān and many things from the sciences of knowledge which many of the scholars have been prevented from.

And:

> If I was offered the amount of gold equivalent to this entire fortress, it would be equal to my gratefulness for this blessing (of being imprisoned).

He reflected over his final imprisonment and said:

> I could never repay them for what has resulted from good to me in it (the prison).[1]

The many instances of Ibn Taymiyyah's exemplary patience have amazed all those who have come to know of the trials he endured in upholding the traditions of the Salaf. To my delight, I came across a treatise entitled *Qāʿidah Fī al-Ṣabr* included in *Jāmiʿ al-Masāʾil* (1/165), a collection of Ibn Taymiyyah's shorter works compiled by our respected Shaykh and Muhaqqiq Muhammad 'Uzair Shams. Although the work is short,[2] it nonetheless contains much benefit and lessons and illustrates Ibn Taymiyyah's psychological disposition, which

---

[1] For references, refer to Muḥammad ibn ʿAbd al-Hādī al-Maqdisī, al-Intiṣār fī Dhikr Aḥwāl Qāmiʿ al-Mubtadiʿīn wa Akhbār al-Mujtahidīn Taqī al-Dīn Abī al-ʿAbbās Aḥmad ibn Taymiyyah.; Shams al-Dīn Muḥammad ibn Abī Bakr Ibn Qayyim al-Jawziyyah, al-Wābil al-Ṣayyib min al-Kalim al-Ṭayyib.

[2] The original treatise Qāʿidah fī al-Ṣabr is thought to be part of a larger work on patience and gratefulness, which is no longer extant. This is indicated by Ibn Taymiyya's introduction, in which he clearly sets out two principles, patience and gratefulness, but only discusses the former. Furthermore, the treatise appears to end abruptly at the mention of the latter principle. If this is indeed a portion of a larger work, then it is likely to be the one referred to by Ibn ʿAbd al-Hādī in *Al-Instiṣār* as *Qāʿidah Fī al-Ṣabr Wa al-Shukr* (The Principle of Patience and Gratefulness). Allah knows best.

strengthened him during his trials and tribulations, and furthermore allowed him to find peace and contentment in situations where most would only fall into despair and depression. Perhaps it will direct us similarly when we face inevitable times of hardship and difficulty.

Written by one in need of Allah's mercy,
Abū Fatimah Azhar Majothi
13-Jumādā al-Ūlā-1435 A.H.
Corresponding to: 15-March- 2014

بِسْمِ اللَّهِ الرَّحْمَٰنِ الرَّحِيمِ

In The Name Of Allah, The All-Merciful, The Bestower Of Mercy

Shaykh al-Islam Ibn Taymiyyah said:

Allah has prepared some good for His believing slaves in every stage (of life): they are always experiencing some blessing from their Lord, whether they encounter what they like or dislike. And Allah has made His judgments and decrees which He ordains and makes possible for them like trade by which they profit from, or pathways by which they are able to reach Him; just as it is affirmed in the *Ṣaḥīḥ*, from the believers' Imām and master (the Prophet [PBUH]), whose name, when every nation will be called by their leaders on the Day of Standing, will be referred to when calling them:

> Amazing is the affair of the believer. Indeed, all of his affairs are good! And that is not for anyone but the believer. If good befalls him, he is grateful, and

so it is good for him; and if harm befalls him, he is patient, and so it is good for him.[3]

This hadith is general and incorporates all of Allah's decrees for His believing slave and indicates that they are something good if a slave is patient when the decree is what is disliked and grateful when it is what is liked. In fact, this concept falls under the title of 'faith' *(Īmān)*, just as some of the Salaf mentioned, that "faith has two halves: one half is patience, and the other is gratitude." This is based on the statement of Allah, the Most High:

﴿إِنَّ فِي ذَٰلِكَ لَآيَاتٍ لِّكُلِّ صَبَّارٍ شَكُورٍ ۝٥﴾

"Indeed, in that are signs for everyone patient and grateful."[4]

If the slave of Allah considers the entire religion, he will see that it returns in its entirety to patience and gratitude. This is because there are three types of patience:

---

[3] Recorded by Muslim (2999).

[4] Surah Ibrāhīm: 5.

The First Type: Patience in carrying out acts of obedience (to Allah)

The slave (of Allah) almost does not carry out the order except after demonstrating some kind of patience, perseverance, and struggle against his inner and open enemy. Thus, his performance of the obligatory duties and recommended ones are according to this patience.

The Second Type: Patience in refraining from prohibitions

Certainly, the soul and its inclinations, Satan's allurement, and bad company all invite and encourage one to sins. Therefore, by the strength of one's patience, one is able to leave them. Some of the Salaf said:

> *"Good actions are carried out by both the good-doer and evil-doer, but no one is able to leave sins except the truthful one."*

The Third Type: Patience with what one is afflicted by, without choice

This is of two types:

1. A type which the creation has no control over, such as sickness and other kinds of God-sent afflictions; such matters facilitate one's patience as he is able to witness in them the decree of Allah and fate, and that people have no ability to alter them. Thereby, a slave of Allah bears patiently whether he is compelled or given a choice.

If Allah opens the slave's heart to the doors of contemplation over the benefits of the affliction and all that it contains of favours and grace, he turns from being patient to being grateful and pleased with it. In truth, the affliction transforms into a blessing, and both his heart and tongue continue to call out: *"My Lord! Help me to remember You, thank You, and worship You well!"*[5]

This condition is either strengthened or weakened in accordance to the strength and weakness of the slave's love for Allah. In fact, we often find this is a reality of life, as the poet said, addressing his beloved (who harmed him in some way), *"Though it grieves me that you defamed me with evil, it pleased me to know that I crossed your mind."*

2. A type which reaches him at the hands of the people with respect to his wealth, honour, or self. This type is very difficult to bear with patience because the soul feels the pain, it dislikes being overpowered, and so it seeks revenge. No one is able to bear this type of affliction with patience except the Prophets and the truthful. When our Prophet was harmed, he would say: *"May Allah have*

---

[5] A prophetic supplication as recorded by Ahmad (5/244), Abū Dawūd (1522), and al-Nasā'ī (3/53).

mercy on Musa! He was afflicted with greater harms than this but bore it with patience!"[6]

And the Prophet informed the people that one of the past Prophets was beaten by his people and said: "*O Allah! Forgive my people, for indeed they know not!*"[7] It has further been reported from the Prophet that something similar happened to him at the hands of his people, and he said (a supplication) like this.[8] There are three matters which are combined in the supplication, namely: pardoning them (the wrongdoers), seeking forgiveness for them, and excusing them for their ignorance.

The end result of this type of patience is victory, honour, happiness, safety, and power in the cause of Allah, in addition to the increase of one's love for Him, the people's love for him (the slave), and an increase of knowledge. Accordingly, Allah, the Most High, states:

And We made of them imams who guided us by Our command when they were patient and were certain of Our remains.

---

[6] Recorded by al-Bukhārī (3150) and Muslim (1062).

[7] Recorded by al-Bukhari (3477) and Muslim (1792).

[8] The supplication was made at the Battle of Uhud and is recorded by al-Tabarani in *al-Muʿjam al-Kabīr* (5694).

﴿وَجَعَلْنَا مِنْهُمْ أَئِمَّةً يَهْدُونَ بِأَمْرِنَا لَمَّا صَبَرُوا ۖ وَكَانُوا بِآيَاتِنَا يُوقِنُونَ ﴿٢٤﴾﴾

"And We made from among them leaders guiding by Our command when they were patient and [when] they were certain of Our signs.[9]"

By patience and certainty, one is able to attain leadership in the religion; if one was to add to this patience, strength of certainty, and faith, he would advance through the levels of happiness by the grace of Allah, the Most High;

﴿ذَٰلِكَ فَضْلُ اللَّهِ يُؤْتِيهِ مَن يَشَاءُ ۚ وَاللَّهُ ذُو الْفَضْلِ الْعَظِيمِ ﴿٢١﴾﴾

"That is the grace of Allah, bestowed on whom He wills, and Allah is the owner of tremendous grace."[10]

This is why Allah, the Most High, states:

---

[9] Surah al- Sajdah: 24.

[10] Surah Hadīd: 21.

﴿ٱدۡفَعۡ بِٱلَّتِي هِيَ أَحۡسَنُ فَإِذَا ٱلَّذِي بَيۡنَكَ وَبَيۡنَهُۥ عَدَٰوَةٞ
كَأَنَّهُۥ وَلِيٌّ حَمِيمٞ ٣٤ وَمَا يُلَقَّىٰهَآ إِلَّا ٱلَّذِينَ صَبَرُواْ وَمَا يُلَقَّىٰهَآ
إِلَّا ذُو حَظٍّ عَظِيمٖ ٣٥﴾

"And thereupon the one whom between you and him is enmity [will become] as though he was a devoted friend. But none is granted it except those who are patient, and none is granted it except one having a tremendous portion.[11]*"*

[11] Surah Fussilat: 34-35.

Many Factors Aid the Slave (Of Allah) In Practising Patience:

1. That one attest to the fact that Allah is the creator of the slaves' actions, their movements, their stationary positions, and their wishes; whatever Allah wills, is; and whatever He wills not, cannot be; no atom in the world, be it the heavens or the earth, moves except by His permission and will. Thus, the slaves are like instruments (yet they have free-will), so look towards the One who empowered them over you and do not look at their (bad) actions towards you, it will relieve you from worry, grief, and sorrow.

2. That the slave (of Allah) attests to his sins, and that Allah has only allowed them (his enemies) control over him due to his sins, just as Allah, the Most High, states:

﴿وَمَآ أَصَٰبَكُم مِّن مُّصِيبَةٍ فَبِمَا كَسَبَتْ أَيْدِيكُمْ وَيَعْفُوا۟ عَن كَثِيرٍ ۝٣٠﴾

"And whatever of misfortune befalls you, it is because of what your hands have earned, and He pardons much.[12]*"*

[12] Surah al- Shūra: 30.

Thus, when the slave attests that everything which reaches him from dislikeable things is caused by his sins, he busies himself with repentance and seeking forgiveness from them due to which he has been overcome by the people's censure, blame, and slander. And when you see a slave affected by people when they harm him, but he does not reproach himself and seek forgiveness, then know that his calamity is truly a great one, but if he repents and seeks forgiveness, saying *"this is because of my sins,"* it turns out to be a blessing in respect to him. Ali b. Abi Talib said a statement which is from the gems of speech: *"Let a slave not have hope in anyone but his Lord [for He alone causes good and repels evil], nor let a slave fear anything but his sin [due to its consequence overpowering him]."* And it is reported from him and others that: *"No calamity befalls a person except due to sin, and it is not lifted except by repentance."*

3. That the slave (of Allah) realises the fact that the best of rewards which Allah has promised is for whoever pardons and is patient, just as He, the Most High, states:

﴿وَجَزَٰٓؤُاْ سَيِّئَةٖ سَيِّئَةٞ مِّثۡلُهَاۖ فَمَنۡ عَفَا وَأَصۡلَحَ فَأَجۡرُهُۥ عَلَى ٱللَّهِۚ إِنَّهُۥ لَا يُحِبُّ ٱلظَّٰلِمِينَ ٤٠﴾

"The Recompense for an evil is an evil like thereof, but whoever forgives and makes reconciliation, his reward is due

from Allah. Verily, He likes not the oppressors, polytheists, and wrong-doers.[13]"

Mankind is of three types in relation to the reciprocation of harm:

i. The oppressor who takes more than his right;
ii. The sparing one who takes the value of his right;
iii. The good-doer who pardons and leaves off his right.

Allah mentioned the three types in this verse, the first part is directed to the sparing ones, its middle to the forerunners (the good doers), and its end to the oppressors.

And a caller will testify on the Day of Standing saying: "*Let him rise whoever's reward is binding upon Allah (to recompense by His will alone)!*"[14], and none will step forward except the one who forgave and made reconciliation. When he (the slave) sees for himself, along with that, that one loses reward due to retaliation and taking (one's right in the world), patience and forgiveness becomes easy for him.

4. That the slave (of Allah) realises the fact that when he forgives and reacts well, it causes him to have open-heartedness towards his fellow brethren, and

---

[13] Sūrah al-Shūra: 40.

[14] Recorded by Ibn Abi Hatim and others.

cleanses him from treachery and holding grudges, seeking retaliation or intending evil. And one obtains the sweetness of pardoning which increases his delight and benefit, be it immediate or in the distant future, over any benefit gained by retaliation. And such a person is included in the statement of the Most High:

﴿وَٱللَّهُ يُحِبُّ ٱلْمُحْسِنِينَ ﴿١٣٤﴾﴾

"Verily, Allah loves the good doers.[15]*"*

Thus, the slave becomes a beloved of Allah, and his condition becomes like one from whom a dirham is taken, but he is compensated with thousands of dinars by which he rejoices in what Allah has bestowed upon him with the utmost joy possible.

5. That the slave (of Allah) acknowledges that nobody ever retaliates for himself except that it causes within him humiliation; and when he pardons, Allah, the Most High, honours him. This is included in what the truthful and trusted one (i.e., the Prophet) informed of, when he said:

> Allah does not increase a slave for his action of pardoning except in honour.[16]

---

[15] Sura Al- Imran: 134.

[16] Recorded by Muslim (2588).

Thus, the honour which one achieves by pardoning is more beloved to him and beneficial than the honour he achieves by retaliating, for indeed this type (which involves retaliation) is honour outwardly but causes shame inwardly, and pardoning may be humiliating inwardly, but it also causes honour inwardly and outwardly.

6. And it is from the greatest benefits: the slave (of Allah) realises that recompense is with its like, that he himself is a sinner, and that whoever pardons people, Allah pardons him, and whoever forgives them, Allah forgives him. Thus, when he realises that his pardoning, excusing, and behaving well with them - despite their ill treatment of him, is a cause of Allah recompensing him with the like of his actions by forgiving him, pardoning him, and doing good to him despite his sins, and in addition to this, pardoning and being patient is made easy for him. And this benefit suffices the intelligent one.

7. That the slave (of Allah) knows that when he busies himself with retaliation and reciprocation, his time is wasted, his heart is divided, and he loses benefits which are not possible to make up for; and perhaps this is harder upon him than the calamity which reached him due to them. Thus, if he pardons and excuses, his heart and body are free to achieve the benefits which are more. important to him than retaliation.

8. That the slave (of Allah's) retaliation, his taking (his right) and his standing up for it, is merely for himself and for his revenge, but indeed the Messenger of Allah [PBUH] would never take revenge for himself; so considering he was the best of Allah's creation and the most noble of them with Allah, he did not take revenge for himself even though harming him was a (futile) attempt to harm Allah and is connected to the rights of the religion, and his self was the noblest, the most pure, most righteous and furthest from every dispraised characteristic, and the most closest to every beautiful characteristic - yet despite this, he did not take revenge. Therefore, how can any of us take revenge for ourselves while knowing the faults and evils within us? In fact, the man who knows his worth, does not consider himself worthy of taking revenge. For him, his self does not have enough value to oblige him to champion his cause.

9. If the slave (of Allah) is harmed because of something he did for the sake of Allah (and which was according to His Sharīᶜah), or for something which he was commanded to do out of obedience to Him or prohibited from doing due to it being disobedience to Him, patience is binding upon him and there is no retribution for him;

he has been harmed for the sake of Allah so his reward is with Allah. Due to this, when the Mujahidūn in the path of Allah lose their blood and wealth for Allah's sake, and these things are not insured, as He has purchased from them their selves and their wealth, it is up to Him to pay the price and not the creation. So, whoever seeks the creation to pay the price, there is no price for Allah to pay for him, for whoever's loss is for the sake of Allah, it is up to Allah to take care of his offspring (and other responsibilities).

And if the slave (of Allah) was harmed due to a sin, then let him turn to himself with blame; and by him blaming himself it will busy him from blaming the one who harmed him. And if he has been harmed in respect to his wealth, then let him resolve to practise patience, for indeed recovering one's wealth is a matter more bitter than having patience. Thus, whoever cannot observe patience over the midday heat, rain, snow, the difficulties of journeys, and highway robbers, then there is no need for him to carry out trading. And this is a matter commonly understood amongst people: that whoever is sincere in seeking something, the patience observed in seeking it is recompensed in proportion to his (level of) sincerity.

10. That the That the slave (of Allah) realises the fact that Allah is with him when he is patient, as well as Allah's love for him and His being pleased with him due to it; so, whoever Allah is with, He repels from him the various kinds of harm and injury which none from His creation can repel. Allah, the Most High, states:

﴿وَٱصۡبِرُوٓاْۚ إِنَّ ٱللَّهَ مَعَ ٱلصَّٰبِرِينَ ٤٦﴾

"And be patient; surely, Allah is with those who the patient ones.[17]"

And Allah, the Most High, states:

﴿وَٱللَّهُ يُحِبُّ ٱلصَّٰبِرِينَ ١٤٦﴾

"...And Allah loves the patient ones.[18]"

11. That the slave (of Allah) realises that patience is half of faith; he should not substitute even a portion of his faith (in Allah) to having faith in aiding himself, for if he practises patience, then he preserves his faith and protects it from decreasing. And Allah the Most High defends those who believe.

12. That the slave (of Allah) realises that his patience is a resolution from him against his own self and

---

[17] Surah al- Anfal: 46.

[18] Surah Al Imran: 146.

an act of his mastery and superiority over it. And when the self is subdued and overpowered by a person, it is not pleased with its subjugation, captivity, or it being thrown into destruction. But when a person is obedient to his self and pays attention to it, and is subdued by it, it continues this way until it destroys him, or the mercy from his Lord reaches him. Therefore, had there been nothing in patience except its mastery over the self and Satan, then it would manifest the heart's authority, establish his soldiers, and he is thereby delighted, strengthened and repels his enemy thereby.

13. That the slave (of Allah) knows that if he practises patience, then Allah will undoubtedly aid him. Certainly, Allah is the guardian over the patient one who defers his oppressor over to Him. But whoever attempts to gain victory by taking a stand for himself, then Allah entrusts him to his own cause, and he remains the only helper to himself. So what comparison is there between the one whose aid is Allah, the best of helpers, and the one whose aid is himself, the most incapable and weakest of helpers?

14. That the slave (of Allah's) patience with the one who harms him and bearing it, in addition to the people rebuking the wrongdoer, leads his opponent to leave oppressing others, feel remorse, and seek pardon.

Thus, the wrongdoer recants after harming the patient person out of shyness and regret over what he committed; moreover, he may also become a supporter to him. And this is the meaning of the statement of Allah, the Most High:

﴿وَلَا تَسْتَوِي ٱلْحَسَنَةُ وَلَا ٱلسَّيِّئَةُ ۚ ٱدْفَعْ بِٱلَّتِي هِيَ أَحْسَنُ فَإِذَا ٱلَّذِي بَيْنَكَ وَبَيْنَهُۥ عَدَٰوَةٌ كَأَنَّهُۥ وَلِيٌّ حَمِيمٌ ﴿٣٤﴾ وَمَا يُلَقَّىٰهَآ إِلَّا ٱلَّذِينَ صَبَرُوا۟ وَمَا يُلَقَّىٰهَآ إِلَّا ذُو حَظٍّ عَظِيمٍ ﴿٣٥﴾﴾

"And not equal are the good deed and the bad. Repel [evil] by that [deed] which is better; and thereupon the one whom between you and him is enmity [will become] as though he was a devoted friend. But none is granted it except those who are patient, and none is granted it except one having a great portion [of good].[19]"

15. Perhaps o Perhaps one's revenge and reciprocation may be a cause for the increase of his evildoing, empowering him and his schemes in afflicting different kinds of harms, which is something witnessed (in our time). If the slave (of Allah) is patient and pardons, he would be secure from this danger, and the intelligent person would never choose the greater of two harms by repelling the lesser. How often has retaliation and

---

[19] Surah al-Fussilat: 34-35.

reciprocation led to an evil which a person then found himself unable to defend himself from? And how often have lives, leadership, wealth, and kingdoms been lost which would have remained, had the oppressed one pardoned?

16. The person who accustoms himself to seeking revenge and not practising patience will inevitably fall into wrongdoing. This is because the soul does not restrict itself to the precise level of justice due to it, unknowingly and unintentionally; perhaps it may also be unable to restrict itself to the required level of upholding the truth, for anger leads a person to an extreme, whereby he does not comprehend what he is saying or doing. Thus, when the slave (of Allah) is the one oppressed, he anticipates support and honour (from Allāh), whereas if he becomes an oppressor, he anticipates Allah's hatred and punishment.

17. This oppression which the slave (of Allah) has suffered is a factor by which either his sins will be expiated, or he will be raised in status. So, if he sought revenge and did not practise patience, it will not be an atonement for his sins, nor an elevation of his status.

18. The slave (of Allah's) pardoning and patience are from the greatest soldiers belonging, to him against his opponent. Certainly, whoever practises patience and pardons, will find they are a cause for his enemy's humiliation and fear, and his dread of him and others, who will not stay silent about his opponent, even if he does. If one retaliates, all of the above is forfeited. Hence, you find many people who, when they curse or harm someone, they love to receive the same treatment back; if the harm is reciprocated, they find ease and cast off the burden they held.

19. If one If one was to pardon his opponent, this would lead the opponent to feel that the victim is superior to him and that indeed he has profited over him (by forgiving him); thus, the opponent does not cease to perceive himself inferior to him. This is sufficient enough as a virtue and honour of pardoning others.

20. If one pardons and forgives, then this is a good deed which will result in another good deed, and that one would result in another good deed and so on and so forth. Thus, the slave (of Allah's) good deeds will never cease to increase, for the reward of doing good is good, just as the recompense of evil is evil. It may also be a factor of his salvation and eternal bliss, but if he was to seek retaliation and avenge himself, then (all of) that would cease to exist.

The second foundation is gratefulness, and it is to work in obedience to Allah, the Most High.

This treatise ends with the praise of Allah the Most High. And may He send peace and blessings on our master Muhammad, his believing household, and Companions.

9 789394 770201

Printed at Repro India Ltd.